How to Study the Bible

by

Ralph Earle

Beacon Hill Press of Kansas City
Kansas City, Missouri

Contents

Preface

Before we take up our discussion of *how* to study the Bible, we should like to look at a preliminary question. It is this: *Why* study the Bible?

Sir Walter Scott lay dying in his home at Abbottsford, England. He called to his friend Lockhart, who was waiting on him, and said, "Bring me the book."

Lockhart glanced at the poet's massive library of books and responded, "Which book?"

Scott's answer was brief: "There's only *one* book—the Bible."

What other book does really matter when one is dying? The Bible shows us the way to heaven—infallibly, unerringly. That is the only thing that matters when one is leaving this world.

But the Bible shows us not only how to die; but also how to live. So we all need to read and study it carefully.

In the prologue to my book *How We Got Our Bible*, we have written:

A lonely shepherd sat on the back side of the desert. All was still. No blaring radio, glaring television, ringing doorbell or telephone. No rumble of distant traffic or roar of jet piercing the sky. Not a sound shattered the silence; not a sight of moving man or beast greeted his eye.

A later psalmist was to write: "Be still, and know that I am God" (Ps. 46:10). In the stillness of that distant day a grateful shepherd met the Great Shepherd. From leading a few sheep of his father-in-law he was called to lead the large flock of God's people.

The solitude lent wings to his thoughts. He remembered the stories his devout mother had told him—of Adam and Eve, of Cain and Abel, of Noah and the Flood, of Abraham, Isaac, Jacob, and Joseph. Little did he realize that under the inspiration of the divine Spirit he would one day be the human instrument for preserving these stories for countless generations to come.

His mind went back over his own lifetime. A cruel Pharaoh had given orders to kill all the male children of Israel. But as a baby, Moses had been miraculously preserved from death. Adopted by Pharaoh's daughter, he had been brought up at the royal palace. There he was carefully educated "in all the wisdom of the Egyptians, and was mighty in words and in deeds" (Acts 7:22 [KJV]). Egypt was the greatest empire of that day and the leading center of learning. God was preparing His servant for his twofold task. The training he received as heir to the throne of the Pharaohs stood him in good stead when he became the founder of the new nation of Israel, and the schooling he had received in the greatest literature of that day was priceless in his preparation for becoming the first scribe of divine Scripture.

1

The New Testament First

You say, "But the Bible begins with Genesis, 'The Beginning.'" Right! But we feel strongly that most Christians would learn better how to study the Bible if they began with the first five books of the New Testament—the four Gospels and Acts—than they would if they started with the five books of Moses: Genesis, Exodus, Leviticus, Numbers, and Deuteronomy. In Exodus and Leviticus, especially, we find very detailed commandments of the Law. So we are going to begin with the New Testament and leave the Old Testament until a later time.

We would suggest that each day you read your chapter for that day. Then go back over the chapter, using whatever study helps you have available.

Before we begin our actual study, perhaps we should deal with the matter of timing. What is the best time to have our quiet reading and studying?

This will differ with different people. Some like to rise early for prayer and Bible reading. Mothers might find the best time after husband has left for work and the children have gone to school.

Undoubtedly there will be many who will have to put it off until evening. But why not spend an hour or two at that time in soul-satisfying Bible study, rather than in watching television? Certainly this would be helpful and valuable for most Christians.

We want first to present a one-year plan for the study of the New Testament, and later a three-year plan for the study of the Old Testament (which is nearly three times as long as the New Testament). That will balance things off in proper shape.

Here is the plan for going through the New Testament in one year. Of course, you can start any month and then continue through the previous month of the following year.

> January—Matthew (a chapter a day)
> February—Mark (Read through twice)
> March—Luke (a chapter a day)
> April—John (roughly a chapter a day)
> May—Acts (a chapter a day)
> June—Galatians and Romans
> July—1 and 2 Thessalonians
> August—1 and 2 Corinthians (a chapter a day)
> September—Prison Epistles (Philemon, Colossians, Ephesians, Philippians)
> October—Pastoral Epistles (1 Timothy, Titus, 2 Timothy)

November—Hebrews and General Epistles (James
—Jude)

December—Revelation

We believe that if you will follow this plan, you will find a fresh thrill in reading and enjoying the New Testament.

I would strongly urge each student to purchase at once the following two books: *The Story of the New Testament* and *Know Your New Testament*. These can be ordered from the Nazarene Publishing House, P.O. Box 419527, Kansas City, MO 64141. Hopefully, they might be found at a local Christian bookstore.

The Story of the New Testament gives a brief introduction to each of the 27 books of our New Testament. This introduction should be read before you begin the study of each book. Then you will understand better the authorship, purpose, and main emphasis of the particular book you are studying at that time.

Know Your New Testament is a brief study of the contents of each book—almost paragraph by paragraph. So you should read the appropriate section each day in the chapter of the Bible for that day.

Before we begin our study of the New Testament in keeping with the plan we have already outlined, we should like to deal briefly with another question. It is this: What version of the Bible should we use?

We would strongly recommend *The Holy Bible, New International Version*, which appeared in 1978 (revised, 1983). The translation was officially made by The Committee on Bible Translation, with the help of over 100 others. All of these men were godly evangelical scholars who subscribed to the infallibility of the Bible as God's inspired Word. As a charter member of that committee we can say without fear of contradiction that the NIV was produced with more thorough, meticulous care than any other version of the Bible that has appeared. We would recommend that the *New American Standard Bible* (1977), also made by godly evangelical scholars, be used along with the NIV for study purposes.

A. The Four Gospels

Matthew has 28 chapters, Luke 24 chapters, John 21 chapters, and Acts 28 chapters. So they will each fit very neatly into the plan of studying one chapter a day for a whole month—allowing for a possible knockout on three or four days! You can think of each of these as your "book of the month" while studying it. Mark (16 chapters) can be read through twice, or you can average half a chapter a day.

At this point we want to make a few suggestions about the four Gospels, and also Acts. Together they will have our attention for 5 out of the 12 months of the year.

Matthew's Jewish name was Levi, and he was a tax collector for the Roman government when Jesus called him (Mark 2:14). So he was despised by the Jewish leaders, especially the Pharisees (vv. 15-16). Yet Jesus appointed him to be one of His 12 apostles (3:13-19). And he it was who wrote this long Gospel, writing it particularly for the Jews.

That is why he begins with Jesus' genealogy, right in the first chapter (vv. 1-17). Unless he could demonstrate that Jesus was a "son of Abraham" (v. 1), a true Israelite, and specifically "the son of David," the Jews would not accept Him as their Messiah. So the genealogy had to come first.

Incidentally, don't bog down by trying to pronounce all these Jewish names. Move right ahead to the birth of Jesus (vv. 18-25).

One of the striking features of Matthew's Gospel is the long discourses of Jesus that are recorded here. We have the Sermon on the Mount (chaps. 5—7), many parables (as in chap. 13), and the Olivet Discourse (chaps. 24 and 25). All of these would be of special interest to the Jews. The Sermon on the Mount is largely a reinterpretation of the Mosaic Law—"You have heard that it was said . . . But I tell you" (5:21-22, 27-28, see 31-32, 33-34, 38-39, 43-44). In chapter 6 Jesus deals at length with giving, praying, and fasting, all of which were emphasized by the Jews of that day. As we would say now, "All these things were right down their alley."

In contrast to Matthew, Mark's Gospel is the "Gospel of Action." That is one reason it is shortest of the four Gospels: It contains relatively few of the teachings of Jesus. It has only 4 of the parables of Jesus, compared to 16 in Matthew and 16 in Luke. (John has no parables.)

Mark was writing for the Romans, who wanted action. While both Matthew and Luke give a genealogy of Jesus, Mark has none. They each have three full chapters of introduction before Jesus begins His public ministry, but Mark has only 13 verses! The Romans didn't care where a man came from; all they wanted to know was what he could do. And that is what Mark presents about Jesus, who walked over Galilee and Judea, performing miracles wherever He went.

Luke was a Greek physician, the only Gentile writer of a New Testament book. He was writing for the Greeks. So instead of giving a Jewish genealogy of Jesus, starting with Abraham (as Matthew does), he starts with Jesus and goes clear back to Adam (3:38). It should be noted that he says Jesus "was the son, so it was thought, of Joseph" (v. 23). This, together with the fact of different names in Luke and Matthew for the same period of time, has led many scholars to maintain that Luke is giving us the actual genealogy of Mary, Jesus' real mother, not that of Joseph, His foster father. His legal genealogy (in Matthew) entitled Him to the throne of David. His actual genealogy, through Mary, while also showing Him descended from David, makes Him one of us.

In line with this we should note that Luke emphasizes the humanity of Jesus more than the other three Gospels do. Part of this is reflected in the fact that Luke gives more attention to women, children, and poor people than the other Gospels. Luke, the beloved physician, had a great appreciation for Jesus as the Friend of human beings.

Matthew, Mark, and Luke are called "The Synoptic Gospels." The term "synoptic" comes from Greek, meaning "seeing together." The first three Gospels present similar pictures of Jesus—going about performing miracles and speaking in parables.

As we have already noted, John's Gospel has no parables. Instead of starting with a genealogy in the early chapters (Matthew and Luke), or the adult Jesus being prepared for His earthly ministry (Mark), John begins with a theological prologue about the divine, eternal "Word" (1:1) who "became flesh" (v. 14). He presents Jesus as "the Lamb of God" (v. 29) and "the Son of God" (v. 49). In John's Gospel Jesus' miracles are always called "signs"; they signified some spiritual truth. For instance, after Jesus fed the 5,000 He declared, "I am the bread of life" (6:35, 48).

This leads us to note that one of the distinctive, exclusive features of John's Gospel is found in the "I ams" that Jesus uttered. As we have already noted, He said, "I am the bread of life" (6:35, 48). He also declared: "I am the light of the world" (8:12); "I am the gate for the sheep" (10:7); "I am the good shepherd" (10:11, 14); "I am the resurrection and the life" (11:25); and "I am the way and the truth and the life" (14:6).

John, the beloved disciple of Jesus, also states the purpose of his writing this Gospel. In 20:30-31 he records: "Jesus did many other miraculous signs in the presence of his disciples, which are not recorded in this book. But these are written that you may believe that Jesus is the Christ, the Son of God, and that by believing you may have life in his name." Not only *belief* in Jesus, but life in Him.

There is another striking contrast between the Synoptic Gospels and the Gospel of John. All three of them give, during the last week of Jesus' life before His crucifixion, the so-called Olivet Discourse (given on the Mount of Olives). It is recorded in Matthew 24; Mark 13; and Luke 21. This discourse deals with the signs of the second coming of Christ.

In place of this, John gives the Last Discourse of Jesus in the Upper Room at the Last Supper, the night before His crucifixion. The main topic of that discourse is the Holy Spirit, "another Paraclete," whom Jesus promised to send to His disciples to be with them. This "Comforter" (KJV) or "Counselor" (NIV) would take His place as their constant Companion and Helper.

B. Acts

The Book of Acts forms the natural—and a very necessary—link between the four Gospels and the 13 Epistles of Paul. Without Acts, we would find it very difficult to understand Paul's Epistles.

Luke is the author of his Gospel and this Book of Acts. Both are addressed to Theophilus, who is called "most excellent Theophilus" in Luke 1:3. So he was probably a Roman nobleman (cf. Acts 26:25).

Luke begins Acts by saying: "In my former book, Theophilus, I wrote about all that Jesus began to do and to teach." That is, in his Gospel Luke had recorded the *works* and *words* of Jesus on earth. Now Luke is going to tell what Jesus *continued* (cf. "began") "to do and to teach" through His Spirit-filled disciples.

Acts 1:8 is the key verse of that book. Jesus said to His apostles: "But you will receive power when the Holy Spirit comes on you; and you will be my witnesses in Jerusalem, and in all Judea and Samaria, and to the ends of the earth."

This verse gives us both the *power* and *program* of the Early Church. The power was the Holy Spirit, and the program was world evangelization.

This verse also gives us the correct outline of the Book of Acts:

Part One: In Jerusalem (chaps. 1—7)

Part Two: In All Judea and Samaria (chaps. 8—12)

Part Three: To the Ends of the Earth (chaps. 13—28)

In the first two parts, Peter is the main character. But in the third and longest part, Paul is the great missionary to the Gentiles. Peter's main ministry was to the Jews in Jerusalem and all Judea. But Paul's was to the Gentiles throughout the Mediterranean world—the "world" of that day.

The Book of Acts forms a constant challenge to the Church of our day. Through the Holy Spirit we must evangelize the world.

C. Paul's Epistles

You may wonder why we have put Galatians first when we come to Paul's Epistles, and why we have placed it with Romans. The answer is that it is rather generally held that Galatians is the first Epistle Paul wrote and that Romans is somewhat of an enlargement of it. He wrote Galatians to meet a crucial problem that had risen in the churches he had founded in the Province of Galatia on his first missionary journey (Acts 13 and 14). Later he wrote the Epistle to the Romans—the Christian believers in Rome—to establish them in their faith in Christ. In both we find a strong emphasis on justification by faith, which the Judaizers were denying in Galatia. This was the foundational doctrine of Paul's preaching the good news of salvation through faith in Jesus Christ. So it is best to study Galatians and Romans together. They have many parallels.

Why did we place 1 and 2 Thessalonians next in our plan? The answer is that many scholars think that 1 Thessalonians may be the earliest of Paul's Epistles, and perhaps the first book of the New Testament to be written. Paul wrote these two Epistles to the Christians at Thessalonica (in Macedonia, northern Greece today), where he had founded a church on his second missionary journey (Acts 17:1-9). First and Second Thessalonians are called "Advent Epistles" because they give major attention to the Second Coming. But 1 Thessalonians also emphasizes the doctrine and experience of entire sanctification (4:3; 5:23). This is an interesting combination: Sanctification and the Second Coming.

There is a passage in 2 Thessalonians that we might comment on. In 2:7 we read in the King James Version: "only he who now letteth will let, until he be taken out of the way." But the Greek text says exactly the opposite: "but the one who now holds it back will continue to do so till he is taken out of the way" (NIV). Today "let" means "allow" or "permit." But the Greek verb here means "restrain" or "hinder," which was a correct meaning for "let" when the King James Version appeared (1611). The sad fact is that in some passages (both OT and NT) the King James Version says the opposite of what the inspired original Hebrew (OT) or Greek (NT) text says. In fact, some 830 words in the

KJV have changed their meaning since 1611, about 200 radically. That is why it is absolutely essential that we have a version today that is in good, clear, understandable, contemporary English. And that is what we find in the *New American Standard Bible* and in the *New International Version.* The NASB is more nearly a literal translation of the original Hebrew and Greek, and so is excellent for study purposes. But since Hebrew and Greek style are very different from contemporary English style, the NIV is better for general use, and most certainly for children and young people. We must have a version that correctly translates the Bible for our day.

Before proceeding further with Paul's Epistles, there is one point that we should probably emphasize. We noted earlier that Matthew, Luke, John, and Acts fit nicely into a "book of the month" situation. Galatians and Romans together do not fall too far short of filling up a month. But 1 and 2 Thessalonians together have only eight chapters—about a fourth of the days of a month.

This will give opportunity for more study in depth and more time for extensive rereading and unhurried meditation on significant passages. Paul's Epistles are worth all the time we can give them, and they will richly reward our intensive, in-depth study.

In the case of our next month's study, we find 16 chapters in 1 Corinthians and 13 in 2 Corinthians. So we move back to the "chapter a day" situation. Fortunately, these two Epistles do not have so many deep theological passages.

In 1 Corinthians Paul is dealing with problems in the church at Corinth. In 1:11 he says: "My brothers, some from Chloe's household have informed me that there are quarrels among you." He discusses this problem of divisions in the church in the first four chapters of the book. In chapter 5 he deals with a bad case of immorality in the church (5:1). In chapter 6 he chides the Corinthians for having lawsuits among believers.

Then in 7:1 he says: "Now for the matters you wrote about." Thereupon he deals with the problems of marriage (chap. 7), food sacrificed to idols (chaps. 8—10), proper conduct in worship (chap. 11), spiritual gifts (chaps. 12—14), the resurrection (chap. 15), and the collection for the saints (chap. 16).

It is more difficult to isolate specific problems in 2 Corinthians. The paragraph headings in the NIV indicate the subjects Paul discusses. He writes with considerable pathos.

Now we come to the Prison Epistles, so called because Paul wrote them while in prison at Rome. Again we have listed them in order of their age.

During Paul's first imprisonment in Rome (A.D. 59-61 or 60-62), a runaway slave named Onesimus evidently looked up Paul in prison in Rome and was converted. Then he realized that in order to be honest he had to return to his master, Philemon. Naturally he was a bit fearful, for in those days a runaway slave who was caught would be killed.

So Paul wrote a letter to Philemon, asking him to receive Onesimus back, and forgive and reinstate him (Philemon 8-21). Then Paul decided to write a letter to the Colossian church, which met in the home of Philemon (Philemon 2). The Epistle to the Colossians is full of beautiful teachings about Christ (chap. 2) and Christian living (chap. 3). It is a precious book that will reward careful study and prayerful rereading of some passages.

On his way back home to Colossae from Rome, Onesimus would get off the boat in the harbor at Ephesus. So Paul evidently decided to write a letter to the church there, which he had founded some years before (Acts 19). This is in some ways the richest book in the New Testament, deeply devotional. One cannot spend too much time meditating on its spiritual wealth. Take time to read it carefully and prayerfully.

There is considerable evidence that Philippians was written near the end of Paul's first imprisonment. The outstanding theological passage in this Epistle is found in 2:5-11. It describes Christ's self-humiliation and exhorts us to have the mind of Christ (v. 5).

The Pastoral Epistles are so called because they are not written to churches but to two pastors—Timothy and Titus. Paul instructs them on how to conduct the affairs of their churches and outlines the duties and responsibilities of officers in the church. The order of writing is: 1 Timothy; Titus; 2 Timothy—the last Epistle Paul wrote (4:6-8).

May I suggest at this point that everyone who plans to go on into the study of the Old Testament should immediately purchase (or order) a copy of the following two books *Meet the Minor Prophets* and *Meet the Major Prophets.* These will be essential for the beginning of your study of the Old Testament. These can be purchased from the Nazarene Publishing House, P.O. Box 419527, Kansas City, MO 64141, if they are not available in your local Christian bookstore.

D. Hebrews

The majority of scholars believe that Paul did not write Hebrews. The old Greek manuscripts have the simple heading: "To the Hebrews."

This book deals with "better things." We find Christ better than the angels (chaps. 1—2), better than Moses (chap. 3). We read about the better rest (chap. 4), the better High Priest (4:14—7:28), the better covenant (chap. 8), the better tabernacle (chap. 9). Here we also have the great faith chapter (chap. 11).

E. General Epistles

Though Paul's Epistles are named after the churches or individuals to whom he wrote, the General

Epistles are named after those who wrote them. James is held to have been the brother of Jesus and the one who presided at the first church council (Acts 15). He is very practical in his teachings on how to live the Christian life.

First Peter gives a strong emphasis on being holy (1:15-16) and on how different groups of Christians are to live (5:1-9). Second Peter emphasizes the Second Coming (chap. 3), as does Jude. These last two have much in common.

John states the purpose of writing his First Epistle: "I write these things to you who believe in the name of the Son of God so that you may know that you have eternal life" (5:13). The key expression of the Epistle is "We know" (2:3, 5; 3:2, 10, 14, 16, 19, 24; 4:13, 16; 5:2, 15, 18, 20). The main thrust of the Epistle is on God's love for us and our obligation to love each other (3:11-24; 4:7-21).

F. Revelation

The Greek word for "Revelation" is *apocalypsis,* from which we get *apocalypse.* The language of the Book of Revelation is highly apocalyptic, and so is interpreted different ways today. This means that we should avoid being too dogmatic in our particular interpretations.

The book divides itself obviously into three parts: past, present, future (Rev. 1:19). The *past* is the vision of

Jesus that John had just seen in chapter 1. The *present* is chapters 2 and 3, where we have the conditions then existing in the seven churches of the Province of Asia. The *future* takes in the rest of the book (chaps. 4—22). What is described there was future in John's time and we think still future in ours.

2

Now the Old Testament

Having worked our way through the New Testament, from Matthew to Revelation, we now want to tackle the Old Testament. We shall find it somewhat more difficult to read and understand, but it will be worth the effort.

The Old Testament may be divided into four sections:

1. The Law (Genesis—Deuteronomy)
2. The Historical Books (Joshua—Esther)
3. The Poetical Books (Job—Song of Songs)
4. The Prophetical Books (Isaiah—Malachi)

The Prophetical Books, in turn, may be divided into two parts: the Major Prophets (Isaiah—Daniel) and Minor Prophets (Hosea—Malachi).

Of all the different parts of the Old Testament, probably the Prophetical Books are the most valuable for Christians. So we plan to start with the Minor Prophets and take the Old Testament sections in reverse order.

A. The Minor Prophets

The student will want by all means to have my book *Meet the Minor Prophets* for this part of his study. It will make clear the inspired messages of each of the 12 Minor Prophets in turn.

Working on our regular schedule of about a chapter a day (with possible gaps), it will take three months to go through the Minor Prophets. The first month we should study Hosea, Joel, Amos, and Obadiah (27 chapters in all). The second month would include Jonah, Micah, Nahum, Habakkuk, and Zephaniah (20 chapters in all). The third month would cover Haggai, Zechariah, and Malachi (20 chapters).

In my *Meet the Minor Prophets* I have covered each of these books very carefully and rather fully. So I am not offering any comments on them here. I believe most students will especially enjoy our treatment of Hosea.

B. The Major Prophets

Now we come to the Major Prophets: Isaiah, Jeremiah, Ezekiel, and Daniel. In Isaiah we find 66 chapters—just over two months, at a chapter a day. But it is followed by Jeremiah with its 52 chapters—under two months of study. The Lamentations (of Jeremiah) comprise 5 chapters. So these together will take care of four months. Then we have Ezekiel (48 chapters) and Daniel (12 chapters), making 60 chapters for another two months of study. That means that we should spend six months (half a year) in our study of the Major Prophets.

Those who follow carefully day by day in *Meet the Major Prophets* will have almost a paragraph-by-paragraph commentary on these four prophetic books, with careful attention given to the distinctive messages of each. For this reason we do not need to make further comments here. Pray for God's blessing as you study each day.

C. The Poetical Books

One of the missing features of the King James Version of the Bible is that it does not use poetic lines in English to represent Hebrew poetry in the Old Testament. Thus the reader misses some of the beauty and flavor of the original. Since the Poetical Books fill a sizable space in the Old Testament, this is of some importance. We might add, of course, that there are numerous poetical passages in the prophetic books, especially in Isaiah and Jeremiah. These should be presented in poetic form.

The Committee on Bible Translation of the *New International Version* was particularly fortunate in having as one of its members an Old Testament scholar who had specialized at a European university in the study of Hebrew poetic form. This gives high quality to the poetry in the NIV.

Job is a very intriguing book. There is no general agreement as to when, where, or by whom it was written. The setting is "the land of Uz" (1:1), but we are not certain as to its location.

We are told that Job "was blameless and upright; he feared God and shunned evil." The author of the book declares: "He was the greatest man among all the people of the East" (1:3).

Then Satan comes into the picture, accusing Job of hypocrisy and insincerity (1:9-11). The Lord allowed Satan to test Job by killing his animals, his servants, and his children (vv. 12-19). But Job remained firm in his faith and in his loyalty to God (vv. 20-22).

Again Satan falsely accused Job (2:4). And again the Lord allowed Satan to test Job even more severely by afflicting his body very cruelly (vv. 7-8). But once again Job remained true (vv. 9-10). He refused to curse God for allowing him to be tormented.

The first two chapters of Job are in prose form, giving the setting for what follows. Except for a brief explanatory passage (32:1-5) and the Epilogue (42:7-17), the rest of the book is poetry.

Much of English poetry—though not the best—is characterized by rhymes at the end of the lines. But this feature does not belong to Hebrew poetry.

The outstanding characteristic of Hebrew poetry is parallelism. It is of three types. The first is *synonymous parallelism,* where two or three adjoining lines say essentially the same thing. This feature is very common in Job's first speech (chap. 3). The lines are connected by thought, not by sound.

The second characteristic is *antithetic parallelism.* Here two adjoining lines say the opposite. This feature is especially prominent in Proverbs, as we shall see when we come to that book.

The third characteristic is *synthetic parallelism.* Here the second line enlarges on the meaning of the first one.

Chapter 3 has Job's first speech. It was given to his "three friends," who had come to "comfort" him in his affliction (2:11). But they proved to be "miserable comforters" (16:2). The bulk of the book is taken up with the back-and-forth speeches of Job and his three friends (chaps. 3—31). The headings in the NIV indicate who is speaking.

When Job had ended his words (31:40), a younger man, Elihu, entered the fray. He berated Job severely (chaps. 32—37). What a long, heartless speech!

Then the Lord "answered Job out of the storm" (38:1), reproving him for some of the things he had said and attitudes he had taken (chaps. 38—39). Job made a very contrite, humble confession (40:3-5). But still the Lord spoke to him out of the storm (40:6), reproving him further (40:7—41:34). In reply to this, Job came through magnificently (42:6).

The Epilogue (42:7-17) tells how God reproved Job's three friends for their speeches and then rewarded Job abundantly for his loyalty. If we feel tested, let's read Job again!

Ask a person, "Who wrote the Book of Psalms?" and probably the answer will be: "David." Actually only about half the Psalms (73) are attributed to David in the headings. Several other writers are named, and some psalms are anonymous (as the first two). So David was not the writer of the whole collection.

The Hebrew Bible divides Psalms into five books, as indicated in the NIV. Book I consists of Psalms 1—41. Here 37 of the 41 psalms have "of David" in the heading, indicating that David was the author. Book II contains Psalms 42—72. Of these 31 psalms, 18 have "of David" and 6 have "of the sons of Korah" (musicians). Several are anonymous. Book III consists of Psalms 73—89. Of these 17, 11 psalms have "of Asaph," 4 "of the sons of Korah," 1 "of David" (86), and 1 "of Ethan the Ezrahite" (89). Book IV contains Psalms 90—106. Of these 17 psalms, 10 have no title, 2 "of David," and 1 "of Moses the man of God" (90). Book V consists of Psalms 107—150. Of these 44 psalms, 15 have "of David" and 15 "a song of ascents" (120—134). The last 5 psalms (146—150) begin and end, very appropriately, with "Praise the LORD" (Hebrew, "Hallelujah").

Psalm 1 has been called "The Psalm of the Two Ways." It draws a sharp contrast between the person who follows the way of the Lord (vv. 1-3) and the one who follows the way of the wicked (vv. 4-5). Then it declares (v. 6):

> "For the LORD watches over the way of the righteous,
> but the way of the wicked will perish."

Incidentally, this is a clear example of antithetic parallelism.

If you read one psalm a day, it would take five months to go through this book alone (150 psalms). We would suggest that you combine two or three of the shorter psalms as you go along.

Due to limitations of space, we shall have to confine our remarks on this book to a few observations. Psalm 19 contains two parts: I. The Revelation of God in Nature (vv. 1-6); II. The Revelation of God in the Bible (vv. 7-13)—a very interesting combination. The psalm ends with a prayer (v. 14) that all of us might well pray every day. Our thoughts as well as our words must be pleasing to God.

In the New Testament Jesus is called "the good shepherd" who gives His life for the sheep (John 10:11), the "great Shepherd" (Heb. 13:20), and "the Chief Shepherd" (1 Pet. 5:4). These functions of Christ are described graphically in a striking trilogy (Psalms 22; 23; 24). Psalm 22 pictures "the good shepherd"—Christ dying on the Cross for our sins. It begins (v. 1) with His cry of despair (Matt. 27:46) and describes the pain and shame of the Crucifixion (vv. 12-18). Psalm 23 paints the "great Shepherd" guiding His sheep and caring for them. Psalm 24 portrays "the Chief Shepherd"—Christ reigning in glory.

These are examples of what are known as Messianic psalms. Others in this category are Psalms 2; 16; 40; 45; 68; 72; 89; 101; 110; 144.

Psalm 51 is the outstanding one of the seven "penitential psalms." Others are Psalms 6; 32; 38; 102; 130; 143.

The shortest chapter in the Bible is Psalm 117, and the longest is Psalm 119 (176 verses). Incidentally, the middle verse of the Bible comes between these two (118:8):

> "It is better to take refuge in the LORD
> than to trust in man."

Psalm 119 is divided into 22 stanzas of 8 lines in each. This is because there are 22 letters in the Hebrew alphabet—all consonants, no vowels! Each stanza is headed by a letter of the Hebrew alphabet, in order. In each stanza all the eight verses begin with the same Hebrew consonant. This is what is called an "acrostic psalm."

Interestingly, the subject of this longest chapter in the Bible is the Word of God. This is indicated by no less than seven recurring terms: law, statutes, ways, precepts, decrees, commands (all in the first stanza), and word.

The 15 "songs of ascents" (Psalms 120—134) were to be sung by the pilgrims on their way up to Jerusalem for the annual feasts. Psalm 121 is a beautiful one to memorize.

The Book of Proverbs begins with this introduction: "The proverbs of Solomon son of David, king of Israel" (1:1). In 10:1 we read: "The proverbs of Solomon." In 22:17—24:34 we have "sayings of the wise." Significantly, 25:1 declares: "These are more proverbs of Solomon, copied by the men of Hezekiah king of Judah"—long after Solomon's death. Chapter 30 begins with: "The sayings of Agur son of Jakeh—an oracle." Finally, the last chapter (31) has the introductory label: "The sayings of King Lemuel—an oracle his mother taught him." Verses 10-31 give a very beautiful description of a wife of noble character—a favorite Scripture passage for Mother's Day.

One of the main characteristics of Proverbs is the emphasis on "wisdom" (chaps. 1—4; 8—9). Especially important is this key statement:

"The fear of the LORD is the beginning of wisdom" (9:10).

Another dominant characteristic is the very wide use of antithetic parallelism. See chapters 10—15, where the second line of most verses begins with "but."

Ecclesiastes is one of the most unique books in the Bible. It evidently was written by Solomon—"the

Preacher" (KJV) or "the Teacher" (NIV), "son of David, king in Jerusalem" (v. 1; cf. v. 12).

The keynote of the whole book is set forth in verse 2. The King James Version reads: "Vanity of vanities, saith the Preacher, vanity of vanities; all is vanity." The *New International Version* has:

> "'Meaningless! Meaningless!'
> says the Teacher.
> 'Utterly meaningless!
> Everything is meaningless!'"

The writer of Ecclesiastes goes on to say that four things are meaningless: wisdom (1:12-18); pleasures (2:1-11); wisdom and folly (2:12-16); toil (2:17-26). He also refers to "this meaningless life of mine" (7:15). He does admonish young people to remember their Creator (12:1). But then he reverts to his key verse (1:2) again in 12:8.

It seems obvious that Solomon wrote these tragic words in the latter part of his life, when his pagan wives had turned his heart away from God (1 Kings 11:4). The wisest man became a fool! This is a book full of warning for all of us.

Song of Songs is one of the most beautiful love songs ever written. In the very first verse it is attributed to Solomon. What a terrific contrast to the cynical pessimism of Ecclesiastes!

The student should read very carefully the footnote in the NIV. It explains that the margin of that version seeks to identify the changes in speakers. "Lover" is used for the man and "Beloved" for the woman, while other speakers are simply identified as "Friends." We should observe the closing warning of the note: "In some instances the divisions and their captions are debatable." There is much difference of opinion here.

This book is full of warnings to us as Christians. In 1:6 the Beloved says that she was made caretaker of the vineyards, but "my own vineyard I have neglected." Are we busy in church work but neglecting the spiritual vineyard of our own heart and our own family?

Again, she says that her lover called to her to rise and go with him (2:10-13). But she evidently didn't want to get up that early. Later she tried in vain to find him and finally succeeded (3:1-4). We must be quick to follow Christ. "Lover" represents Christ, and "Beloved" the Church.

To be sure that you have the study books in time to use, I would like to suggest at this point that you purchase (or order from the Nazarene Publishing House, Box 419527, Kansas City, MO 64141) five very helpful books in the *Beacon Small-Group Bible Studies:*

> *1 and 2 Samuel,* by A. F. Harper
>
> *Ezra/Nehemiah,* by C. Neil Strait
>
> *Genesis, Part 1,* by Bob Branson
>
> *Genesis, Part 2,* by Ken Bible
>
> *Exodus,* by Earl Wolf

You can also order Frances Simpson's *Ruth/Esther,* which you will need especially for the study of these two fantastic books on how God blessed two women who were faithful to Him.

D. The Historical Books

This section includes no less than a dozen books (Joshua—Esther). Because of lack of space, we shall have to give very brief comments on these.

Joshua divides itself naturally into two sections: the conquest of Canaan (chaps. 1—12), and the division of the land among the 12 tribes (chaps. 13—24). One of the most inspiring passages in the book is 1:6-9. Here God exhorts Joshua, Moses' successor, "Be strong and courageous," and promises him success. This passage could well be memorized.

In sad contrast, Judges is a record of disobedience and defeat (see NIV heading at 2:6). In mercy God raised up a succession of judges, from Othniel (3:7) to Samson (chaps. 13—16). The main lesson of this book is that sin always brings divine punishment, but God is ready to forgive those who repent.

The Book of Ruth is a gem, one of the most beautiful love stories in the Bible. Ruth was brought up in pagan Moab. When her Hebrew husband died, she followed her mother-in-law back to Bethlehem. She was richly rewarded by getting a godly husband and becoming the great-grandmother of King David (4:17), and so the ancestress of Christ (Matt. 1:5, 16). Read about *Ruth* in Frances Simpson's book *Ruth/Esther.*

The most important passage in Ruth is 1:16-17. This should by all means be memorized.

In the Hebrew Bible, 1 and 2 Samuel were just one book. The same was true with 1 and 2 Kings and 1 and 2 Chronicles. But when the Septuagint (Greek) translation of the Old Testament was made about 200 years before Christ, Samuel, Kings, and Chronicles each had to be divided into two books. This was because the Hebrew language had no vowels, but the Greek did. So the text became too long for a single scroll, and each of the three books had to be divided in two.

Samuel was the last of the judges over Israel (1 Sam. 7:15) and the first of the prophets after Moses (2 Chron. 35:18). He was also a priest (1 Sam. 2:18). The story of his birth, childhood, and call (1 Samuel 1—3) is especially fascinating and spiritually uplifting. It should be read carefully.

First and Second Samuel describe the shift from judgeship to kingship in Israel. First we have Samuel as judge (through chap. 7). Then we find Saul as king (1 Samuel 8—31; 2 Samuel 1), and finally David as king (2 Samuel 2—24). These are among the most interesting books to read in the entire Old Testament. The differences between Saul and David form a very dramatic, unforgettable story, which can be of great spiritual blessing.

First and Second Kings describe the reigns of the kings of Judah and Israel. First Kings 1:1—2:11 gives the story of David's final days and death (930 B.C.).

The two books (as we have them) may be divided as follows: Solomon's Reign (1 Kings 1—11); Kings of Israel and Judah (1 Kings 12—2 Kings 17); Kings of Judah Until the Exile (2 Kings 18—25). In 722 B.C. the Northern Kingdom of Israel came to an end with the Assyrian Captivity. In 586 B.C. Jerusalem was destroyed and the Southern Kingdom of Judah ended with the Babylonian Captivity. Since then no Israelite kings have reigned over the people of Israel.

The two Books of Kings present a graphic portrayal of the divine rewards of the righteous and the sad punishments of the wicked. They should help all of us to obey God and enjoy His blessings.

First and Second Chronicles are thought to have been written by Ezra about 450 B.C. They give more attention to spiritual evaluation of the reigns of good and bad kings than do 1 and 2 Kings.

The first nine chapters of 1 Chronicles give very lengthy genealogies to assist the people after the Babylonian Captivity in identifying their family descent. We would suggest that you skim over these chapters quickly. We have known only one man who said he got "blessed" trying to pronounce all these names!

Chapter 10 relates the sad suicide of Saul. Then we have David's wonderful reign (chaps. 11—29). One can find much spiritual inspiration here. The glory of Solomon's reign is described interestingly in 2 Chronicles 1—9, followed by the history of the Southern Kingdom of Judah (2 Chronicles 10—36).

Due to strictures of space, we cannot discuss Ezra and Nehemiah. But you will find adequate material in Neil Strait's excellent book, *Ezra/Nehemiah.* For Esther you will use Frances Simpson's *Ruth/Esther.*

E. The Law

Now we turn to the first main section of the Bible: the Law. This consists of five books: Genesis, Exodus, Leviticus, Numbers, and Deuteronomy. The Hebrew tradition, held by evangelical Christians today, is that all five were written by Moses.

Genesis is the Greek word for "beginning." The student will want to read carefully *Genesis, Part I:* "How It All Began," by Bob Branson.

Chapters 1—4 deal with creation, including that of Adam and Eve, and the fall of man. Chapter 5 traces the human family from Adam to Noah. Then we have the fascinating story of the Flood (chaps. 6—8), God's covenant with Noah (chap. 9), and the descendants of Noah (chaps. 10—11). So the first 11 chapters are, in a sense, introductory.

Now we come to the wonderful story of Abraham (12:1—25:11). He was to be the father of God's chosen people, and the Messiah (Christ) would be "the son of

Abraham" (Matt. 1:1). The next section of Genesis (25:19—36:43) deals with Jacob and Esau.

The rest of the book (chaps. 37—50) is devoted to the story of Joseph. He rivals Abraham for the honor of being the leading character in Genesis. Almost exactly the same space (14 chapters) is devoted to each. While Abraham was the chosen ancestor of Christ, as we just noted, Joseph is probably the outstanding *type* of Christ in the Old Testament. We once listed *38* ways in which Joseph is a type of Christ. That could probably not be done with any other person in the Bible. The study of his life is a constant inspiration. Almost all the other outstanding characters in the Old Testament—Adam, Noah, Abraham, Isaac, Jacob, Moses, David, Solomon, and others—made serious mistakes. But no fault in Joseph's life is recorded in the sacred narrative.

The word *Exodus* comes from the Greek *exodos,* which means "a going out." It records the going out of the children of Israel from Egypt, the giving of the Law at Sinai, and the building of the Tabernacle (see *Exodus,* by Earl Wolf).

Leviticus is so called because it gives detailed directions for the duties of the preists and Levites. Chapters 1—7 give a thorough description of each of the offerings and sacrifices that were to be offered in the Tabernacle. It is interesting to note that the longest space is devoted to the sin offering (4:1—5:13).

Then we have the duties of the priests (chaps. 8—10). This is followed by what is known as the Holiness Code (chaps. 11—22). Here we find one of the most important commands of the Old Testament: "Be holy, because I am holy" (11:44-45; 19:2; cf. 20:7). This is quoted and applied to us as Christians in 1 Pet. 1:16. The rest of Leviticus is taken up with the feasts (chap. 23) and final promises and warnings (chaps. 24—27).

Numbers is so called because it lists two numberings of the Israelite fighting force (1:2-46; 26:2-51). In the Hebrew Bible the title of this book is "In the Wilderness." This is because it describes the wandering of the Israelites for 40 years in the desert of Sinai.

Deuteronomy is from the Greek *deuteros,* "second," and *nomos,* "law." This book relates the second giving of the law—to the Israelites just before they entered Canaan. We find three discourses of Moses—chapters 1—4; 5—26; 27—30. Then we have his final warnings and blessings (chaps. 31—34).